Community Helpers

School Bus Drivers

by Dee Ready

Content Consultant:
Karen E. Finkel, Executive Director
National School Transportation Association

Bridgestone Books
an imprint of Capstone Press

Bridgestone Books are published by Capstone Press,
151 Good Counsel Drive, P.O. Box 669, Mankato, Minnesota 56002.
www.capstonepress.com

Library of Congress Cataloging-in-Publication Data
Ready, Dee.
    School bus drivers/Dee Ready.
    p. cm.—(Community helpers)
    Includes bibliographical references and index.
    Summary: Explains the dress, tools, training, and work of school bus
drivers as well as special features of their buses.
    ISBN 1-56065-560-7 (hardcover)
    ISBN 0-7368-8461-0 (paperback)
    1. Bus drivers—Juvenile literature. 2. Bus driving—Vocational guidance—
Juvenile literature. [1. Bus drivers. 2. School buses. 3. Occupations.] I. Title.
II. Series: Community helpers (Mankato, Minn.)
HD8039.M8R43   1998
371.8'72--dc21
                                                                    97-2957
                                                                    CIP
                                                                    AC

Photo credits
International Stock/Rae Russel, 18
Maguire PhotoGraFX, cover, 6, 8, 14
Unicorn Stock/Andre Jenny, 4; Jean Higgins, 10; Daniel Olson, 12;
   C. Boylan, 16; Tom McCarthy, 20

Table of Contents

School Bus Drivers

School bus drivers take children to and from school. They stop at bus stops. A bus stop is a place where people wait for buses. Sometimes school bus drivers drive buses for school trips, too.

What School Bus Drivers Do

School bus drivers must drive buses safely. They are careful on the road. They look for trains at train crossings. They make sure children get on and off their buses safely.

What School Bus Drivers Wear

Some school bus drivers wear uniforms. Others wear their own clothes. Some drivers wear jackets to keep warm.

Tools School Bus Drivers Use

School bus drivers use a red stop sign. They also use flashing red lights. The lights and stop sign are parts of the bus. They tell other drivers to stop. This is so children can enter or leave the bus safely.

What School Bus Drivers Drive

School bus drivers drive school buses. A school bus has two rows of seats. It has a walkway between the rows. A school bus can carry many children.

School Bus Drivers and School

School bus drivers take classes to learn driving rules. They learn about the parts of buses. They practice driving buses. Then they take a test to become bus drivers.

Where School Bus Drivers Work

School bus drivers drive buses in all communities. They drive buses in cities and in towns. They drive them in the country, too.

People Who Help School Bus Drivers

Dispatchers help school bus drivers. A dispatcher is someone who talks to drivers over a radio. Some people fix buses. Other people wash buses that are dirty.